Transportation

Careers for Today
Transportation

Marjorie Rittenberg Schulz

Franklin Watts

New York • London • Toronto • Sydney

Developed by: Ω Visual Education Corporation
Princeton, NJ

Cover Photograph: George Hall/Woodfin Camp & Associates

Photo Credits: p. 3 George Hall/Woodfin Camp & Associates; p. 6 Tom Tracy/The PhotoFile; p. 11 Chevron Corporation; p. 12 Burlington Northern Railroad; p. 14 Sepp Seitz/Woodfin Camp & Associates; p. 20 Robert Bruschini/Studio B; p.26 Audrey Gottlieb/ Monkmeyer Press Photo Service, Inc.; p. 29 Bob Burch/Bruce Coleman, Inc.; p. 32 William Strode/Woodfin Camp & Associates; p. 35 United States Navy; p. 36 George Post; p. 38 Ken Sherman/ Bruce Coleman, Inc.; p. 44 Texaco, Inc.; p. 48 Eastern Airlines; p. 50 Jacques Chenet/Woodfin Camp & Associates; p. 56 New Jersey Transit; p. 62 United States Navy; p. 65 California Maritime Academy; p. 68 Robert Bruschini/Studio B; p. 74 David Vinyard/ Nawrocki Stock Photo; p. 80 United States Army

Library of Congress Cataloging-in-Publication Data

Schulz, Marjorie Rittenberg.
Transportation/Marjorie Rittenberg Schulz.
p.   cm. — (Careers for today)
Includes bibliographical references (p.   ).
Summary: Describes the various careers available in the
transportation industry and provides suggestions for students
interested in obtaining such work.
ISBN 0-531-10974-7
1. Transportation —Vocational guidance — Juvenile literature.
[1. Transportation — Vocational guidance. 2. Vocational guidance.] I. Title
II. Series: Schulz, Marjorie Rittenberg. Careers for today.
HE152S418   1990
388'.023'73 — dc20   90-12248 CIP AC

Contents

Introduction

Since the invention of the wheel thousands of years ago, people have had transportation on their minds. We have always needed to move people and goods from one place to another. Today we have more and better types of transportation to choose from than ever before.

We buy or rent cars, vans, and trucks to take us and our belongings where we want to go. These vehicles bring the school basketball team to the play-offs, take students to the senior prom, transport travelers to the airport, and get job applicants to interviews on time.

We use public transportation such as buses, trains, subways, and trolleys to shuttle us around town to work, shopping, and ballparks. We look to long-distance buses and trains to provide comfortable travel across the country.

We depend on trucks, airplanes, and trains to transport cargo throughout our nation. We look to ships and planes to bring imported goods from other countries and send our products to other parts of the world.

Reliability is important to all forms of transportation, whether packages or people are being moved. People count on trains, buses, and planes to get their presents delivered in time for Christmas and their families brought to Disney World on schedule.

Without efficient transportation, our country would come to a stop. Just what do transportation workers do to keep us moving?

Transportation Today

More than 3 million people work in transportation. The jobs are on many different levels and require different degrees of training. The airline pilot's job is one of the most demanding in the industry. People must log 1,500 hours of flying time to be commercial airline pilots. Other jobs require less rigorous training or offer it on the job. Many jobs in the industry, such as pilot or radio tower operator, require that the worker have some sort of license from a government agency. To get such a license, the worker must pass a test.

Air transportation offers jobs for flight attendants, pilots, aircraft mechanics, freight and baggage handlers, and other airline employees.

In water transportation, career choices include Merchant Marine engineer, boat and ship mechanic, dockworker, ordinary and able seaman, cook, and steward.

Railroad transportation includes positions such as railroad signaler, telegraph operator, dispatcher, railroad braker, and conductor.

In road and public transportation, openings include bus driver, truck driver, freight handler, mechanic, car rental agent, and more.

The wide variety of jobs in transportation offers many opportunities to young people starting out. They should look for jobs that suit their skills and interests.

Many jobs in transportation give experience that can be used in other fields as well. Clerical workers and sales and marketing representatives, for instance, learn skills that they can apply in many fields.

8

Outlook for the Future

In recent years, transportation has changed greatly. For years, the federal government closely regulated such activities as trucking and airline service. But the 1980s saw a movement to deregulation, or the end of close government supervision of these industries. As a result, the industries have undergone many changes, some of which affect employment.

The number of airlines, for instance, has gone down. At the same time, competition has heated up. Companies trying to get more business have had to cut back on hiring or hold back on wages to keep their costs down.

Deregulation has also helped small companies start up, which has created some new jobs. So the overall outlook for most jobs in transportation is good. The table below shows the fastest- and slowest-growing jobs up to the year 2000.

FASTEST- AND SLOWEST-GROWING JOBS: PROJECTED CHANGE IN EMPLOYMENT, 1986–2000

Fastest-Growing Jobs:

Airplane pilot	29%
Diesel mechanic	23%
Motorcycle mechanic	21%
Boat motor mechanic	21%

Slowest-Growing Jobs:

Auto-body repairer	12%
Air-traffic controller	8%
Gas station attendant	1.6%

Air Transportation

Airline deregulation began in 1978, and the airlines were then able to compete with one another more freely. They fought price wars and made special offers to attract passengers. No longer did the giant commercial airlines get all the business. Many commuter airlines that traveled between small cities started up. Large airlines began to offer more flights to popular destinations.

All these changes created more jobs in the transportation industry. Transportation careers in the armed forces grew. Commercial airlines hired more pilots. And more jobs with private companies opened up. In fact, private corporations drove up the demand for pilots. Many pilots preferred flying for private companies since the schedules were easier, and the pay was good. About 30,000 businesses own or lease airplanes for company travel. The National Business Aircraft Association has nearly 12,000 pilot members.

Large and small airports are expanding to handle the growing flight demand. There will be a greater need for workers to service passengers and maintain aircraft. This means more openings for flight attendants, baggage and freight handlers, and aircraft mechanics in the future.

Water Transportation

Water was one of the first and most often-used types of transportation. People used rivers to bring cities and towns closer together. They sailed from other countries on ships in search of a better life. They shipped goods across oceans.

Ships, such as this oil tanker, bring many of the goods we import from other countries.

Water transportation is still important today for transporting grain, oil, and coal from one continent to another. The future of the shipping industry, however, may not be as bright as that of other areas of transportation. Ships from other countries provide great competition, and new ships are in little demand.

With more automation—machines doing the work that people performed—jobs in shipping will grow very little in future years. Ships will require smaller crews in the future. The U.S. Merchant Marine has already cut many jobs.

Railroad Transportation

The popularity of the railroads has also dropped. Train travel used to be the main way to get from one coast to the other. Today only 1 percent of train travel involves passengers. Most railroads concentrate on transporting freight, an important industry in our country today.

Railroads today do not need as many workers to run them as they once did. In the 1920s, railroads employed more than 2 million people. Today only about 300,000 people work for railroads. With the slow economy of the past years and the rise of deregulation, only the largest, most efficient railroads have stayed in business.

With computers and automated systems replacing clerks and other workers, jobs in the railroad industry do not look promising for the future.

The majority of railroad jobs are in freight rather than passenger service.

Road and Public Transportation

Cars, trucks, buses, and other kinds of road transportation answer many needs today. Trucks and buses are often the only way to transport goods to smaller towns across the country. We also depend on trucks to move goods long distances.

A major part of transportation is the auto industry. Nearly 120 million cars travel our country's roads. Pollution devices, seat belts, air bags, and other advances, plus tougher laws for drunk drivers, have made driving safer today than ever before.

Jobs in some areas of the auto industry will increase in the years ahead. Since auto parts last longer, workers will be needed to service them. About 900,000 people work as auto mechanics. Nearly 180,000 more service buses and trucks. They work for service stations, car dealers, repair shops, auto makers, leasing companies, and the government.

Public transportation moves huge numbers of people every day in cities or from one town to another. Public transportation is largely supported by local, state, and the federal governments. Mass transit has grown tremendously since the mid-1970s. Buses are the most-used form of mass transit.

Competition among bus companies has created more jobs. Commuter and inner-city bus lines and school bus services will need workers in the future. The number of jobs in public transportation will increase steadily in the future, although budget constraints on governments may affect that growth.

Chapter 1
Airline Freight Handler and Dockworker

Airline Freight Handler

Airline travelers have a lot of things to plan and remember: packing everything they need, buying tickets, meeting schedules, making hotel arrangements, and handling a million other details. One thing they do not want to worry about is whether their luggage will be at the airport when they get off the plane at their destination. Making sure that the baggage arrives is the job of the airline freight and baggage handler.

Education, Training, and Salary   No formal education is required for the job of airline freight and baggage handler. Some employers may prefer a worker with a high school education. Workers are trained on the job for this work.

Handlers start out at about $12,000 to $15,000 a year. Beyond that, salary generally depends on how long the handler has held the job. Handlers with several years' experience can earn $17,500 or more a year. Baggage and freight handlers who join unions may earn more. Benefits include health insurance, paid vacations, and retirement plans.

Job Description   Baggage and freight handlers work at airports loading and unloading luggage and cargo. They may also weigh freight and write up shipping orders. They transport passengers' luggage in trailers pulled by jeeps.

Handlers on the ground place luggage on large conveyor belts that travel up to the plane. Another handler, inside the plane, unloads the luggage and sorts it in the baggage storage area. Since some passengers will be getting off at the first stop, their luggage is stored separately from those continuing on to the plane's final destination.

When a plane arrives, handlers drive trailers up to planes to unload luggage and cargo. They work quickly and carefully to get all pieces needed at this destination. They transport the luggage across the field to the airport building. There the luggage is sent up another conveyor belt to the baggage claim area, where passengers get their bags.

If there is a large amount of baggage, the handlers load it into big containers using lifting machines. This enables the handlers to move many bags at a time into the airplane without lifting them one by one.

Outlook for Jobs   With experience and a good work record, an airline freight handler can move up to a job as a manager or supervisor in charge of other workers. Some supervisory jobs require more training.

There should be jobs available in the coming years for airline freight and baggage handlers. Like other jobs in the airline industry, these jobs depend on the state of the economy. If business is

16

Talking About the Job

People always ask me if I have a lot of stories to tell about working at the airport. Well, I have to admit I do have my share.

I'm Theo Racine, and I'm a baggage and freight handler here at Denver-Stapleton Airport. There are quite a few of us since it is a pretty busy place. Lots of people traveling around the country come through Denver—and here in Colorado we get a big share of skiers and other vacationers.

I work wherever I'm needed at the time. Sometimes it's out on the field driving the trailers. Sometimes it's transferring bags to the baggage claim area where passengers come to pick them up.

We have our share of "orphans"—bags that don't get claimed. These are kept for a while by the airline baggage department, but they're impossible to trace with no name tag. Sometimes bags get damaged.

Often these are older ones that are overstuffed and pretty worn out. The airlines try to repair or replace them immediately.

I got my job by applying at the airline office. I went down, filled out an application, and was called back a week later for an interview. A few months later an opening came up, and I got the job. That was nearly five years ago.

Over the years, some things have happened that even I wouldn't have believed. One story is my favorite—I always tell it. I was lifting bags onto the conveyor at the baggage claim. Bags that aren't claimed keep moving around the belt and back through our loading area. But I wasn't ready for the little three-year-old who was riding on top of a suitcase as it came around the curtain! He looked at me as he moved along and said, "This is fun!" I don't think it was as much fun when his father found him!

good and a lot of people are traveling, more handlers will be needed. If the economy slows down, airlines may have to lay off workers. This would mean fewer jobs.

Dockworker

Dockworkers are sometimes called *longshore-men*. They load and unload cargo from ships. They lift cargo by hand or use machines to do the lifting.

Education, Training, and Salary   As with airline baggage handlers, no formal education is required for a dockworker's job. Training takes place on the job. Dockworkers earn average wages of $15.00 to $17.00 per hour, but the rate varies from region to region. Workers receive premiums for overtime, night work, and other special situations. Wages may be covered by a union contract.

Job Description   Dockworkers perform many different duties. Some check and inspect the cargo. They may log in the name of the ship that delivered it, the contents of the cargo, and its size and weight. They must make note of any damage to cargo.

All shipping and receiving invoices and papers go through a checker as well. They are then given to the truck driver, who hauls the cargo to its final destination. Careful attention to detail is important to make sure that shipping records are accurate.

Dockworkers work in groups, or gangs, for each job. One or more longshoremen stand in the hold of the ship to begin unloading cargo. Another operates a winch, or large crane, to lift the cargo from the ship to the dock. The same process is used for loading, but in reverse. Other dockworkers are in charge of repairing the equipment.

Safety is a big factor for dockworkers. Lifting and moving heavy cargo can be a dangerous job, so workers must be trained correctly. They work outside in all weather conditions.

Outlook for Jobs   Job opportunities are different in each area of the country. The largest and busiest ports—New York, New Orleans, and Philadelphia—have the largest numbers of dockworkers. Cities located on the Great Lakes are increasing their shipping capabilities. So more dockworkers may be needed there. Some jobs have been lost to the use of machines. But some openings will always occur as workers change jobs or retire.

For more information on airline freight handlers and dockworkers, write to:

Air Transport Association of America
1709 New York Avenue, NW
Washington, DC 20006
(202) 626–4000

National Freight Transportation Association
P. O. Box 16219
Rocky River, OH 44116
(216) 331–6064

People interested in airline freight and baggage handler jobs should also apply to airline offices, which are listed in the yellow pages. Most dockworker jobs require joining a union, so those interested should register with the union. Some private companies may hire non-union workers.

Chapter 2
Truck Driver

Truck drivers pick up and deliver goods within towns and cities or across the country. They help businesses in all areas provide important services and goods. They deliver milk and mail, bring supplies to construction sites, carry clothing to department stores, and move families' belongings to their new homes. Truck drivers keep America moving day after day.

Local Truck Driver

Education, Training, and Salary   A local truck driver may be required to have a high school education. He or she must have a driver's license and may be required to be twenty-one years old. Drivers can earn between $10.00 and $12.00 per hour.

Job Description   Local truck drivers carry loads within towns and cities or over short distances to nearby areas. They are often hired to take goods from a warehouse or storage facility to a store. Drivers may work alone or have helpers for larger loads.

Some drive light trucks of less than three tons. These include milk delivery trucks, mail trucks, or trucks for small service companies. Driving these trucks is close to driving cars or vans and does not require special driving skills.

Some drivers operate heavy trucks for places like warehouses, or they drive cement mixers or dump trucks. These trucks have several controls, lifts, and ramps to operate.

Drivers may be employed by companies that deliver their own products. Or they may be hired by independent trucking firms that are themselves hired by companies or by individuals. Many local truck drivers are in business for themselves. They may own one or more trucks and hire out for specific jobs.

Local drivers usually receive daily delivery assignments, which come with shipping and receiving papers. The drivers are often responsible for loading merchandise in a careful order or following special handling instructions.

Some companies expect drivers to be able to make minor repairs on their trucks. So mechanical knowledge of trucks is very helpful.

If goods are delivered to a customer's home, the driver unloads the order and takes it into the house. The driver must have the customer sign a receipt saying that the goods were received. The driver may accept payment for COD (cash on delivery) items.

Outlook for Jobs   Drivers can move up to heavy trucks or long-haul trucks. With experience, some become truck dispatchers or supervisors. Some drivers start their own companies. They need business skills.

The future looks good for people interested in becoming local truck drivers. There will be competition for jobs, however, since the position is growing in popularity.

Long-Haul Truck Driver

Education, Training, and Salary   Most companies do not require long-haul truck drivers to have a formal education. Long-haul drivers must be at least twenty-one years old and in good physical health. They must pass a driving test and a written exam on safety regulations. And they must have a commercial driver's license. Some companies require drivers to have several years of experience and to be at least twenty-five years old. Most long-haul drivers have local truck-driving experience. Some have attended technical schools to become trained in long-distance truck driving.

Companies often train new drivers. New drivers will probably make their first trip with an experienced driver to teach them. They must learn to stay alert while driving long distances. And they must learn how to maintain and refuel the truck and what to do in an emergency.

The number of hours worked and the distance driven determine salary. Earnings also depend on the kind of freight and type of truck. Drivers of materials that burn easily are paid more because of the risk. The average salary is $21,000 a year. Benefits include medical insurance, paid vacations, and retirement plans.

Job Description   Long-haul truck drivers transport goods across long distances, often from coast to coast. They drive flatbed trucks delivering steel. They drive tank trucks transporting fuel. They drive tractor trailers loaded with new cars. They drive moving vans filled with a family's furniture and belongings.

Talking About the Job

Driving is what I like. I like the feel of the open road. I like the time to think. And I like listening to my music. I'm Norm Nesforn, and I'm a long-haul trucker for Continental Transport with my wife Cindy. We've been a driving team since 1987, and we always say it's the only life for us. I guess we are independent people, so this is like being our own boss, although we do have to report to the company.

We both had a lot of driving experience before we got hired by Continental. My first job was for a furniture store making deliveries. That was one of the most physical jobs I've ever had. There was a tremendous amount of heavy lifting and carrying every day. But it was good for me, and I knew it was good experience for long-distance hauling.

Cindy worked for a large construction company driving trucks and working heavy equipment. She took several courses in truck maintenance and repair at Hasbrook Tech, so she's trained to drive them and fix them. It's good to have a partner to share the driving, especially when we have to drive a load to Oregon or California from New Jersey.

We have deadlines for delivery, so we don't have much free time. If the boss says it has to be in Portland on Wednesday morning, we'd better get it there. When we are hungry, tired, or need some supplies, the best thing we can see ahead of us is a truck stop. They are really set up for truckers, with a restaurant, showers, fuel, and convenience stores. And we can park the rig there overnight and catch some sleep before we start out again.

It's a good life for us. Someday we plan to have our own rig. Then we'll glide down the highway in our own office without walls.

Long-haul truck drivers must be very experienced and have excellent driving records. They are in charge of expensive trucks and valuable freight. If anything should happen to either truck or freight, the driver is held responsible.

Outlook for Jobs   Long-haul drivers may start out as substitutes for regular drivers. Then they may move up to their own route as they gain experience and seniority. Some drivers may become supervisors or dispatchers.

The future looks good for those interested in becoming long-haul truck drivers. Nearly 2.5 million truck drivers carry one-quarter of the nation's freight. This number is expected to increase by about 20 percent in the coming years. So there will be many openings for people interested in entering the truck-driving profession.

For more information on local truck drivers and long-haul truck drivers, write to:

American Trucking Association
2200 Mill Road
Alexandria, VA 22314
(703) 838–1700

International Brotherhood of Teamsters, Chauffeurs, Warehousemen and Helpers of America
25 Louisiana Avenue, NW
Washington, DC 20001
(202) 624–6800

Many truck drivers belong to unions, so interested people can check in the phone book for one of those organizations. People can also apply directly to local retail or wholesale companies for driving jobs. They should also check the classified ads in the newspaper for job openings.

Chapter 3
Bus Driver

Buses make it easy to travel at affordable prices. People depend on public bus transportation in cities to get to and from jobs, to shopping areas, or to restaurants. Private bus lines that provide trips to other states and areas of the country are less expensive than airlines and trains.

Education, Training, and Salary

Some employers may prefer workers to have a high school education. Bus drivers must be at least twenty-one years old and have a driver's license. Some states require a commercial driver's license also. Drivers must pass a written test and a driving test.

New drivers are trained in the classroom by most companies. They learn about safety rules. They are also given practical, on-the-road training. Beyond that, there may be a training period of one to three months for drivers to get used to the job. New drivers may start out learning from experienced drivers, often beginning as substitutes. Substitute drivers are on standby and work only when route drivers are sick or on vacation.

Local bus drivers' salaries differ in each area of the country. In the Midwest, drivers earn from $13,500 to $20,000 a year. Bus drivers in the northwestern U.S. earn from $19,500 to $25,000 a year. Benefits include medical insurance, paid vacations, and retirement plans.

Intercity bus drivers earn from $22,500 to $26,000 a year. Substitute drivers may be paid by the hour when they are on duty but not actually on the road. They are paid by the mile when they are driving. Drivers get overtime pay when they work extra hours. Meals and lodging are paid for when drivers are out of town overnight. Benefits include medical insurance, paid vacations, and retirement plans.

Job Description

Local bus drivers operate buses within cities and towns. These buses are owned by the city. Some government agencies and private companies also hire bus drivers for transportation.

Local bus drivers work shifts, picking up their buses at the garage when their shift begins. They make sure that the buses are operating correctly, and they pick up any transfer or refund forms they may need. They drive to the bus terminal or to their first stop. Drivers collect fares and help passengers by answering their questions. Drivers must have an idea of the entire system's routes because passengers rely on them for advice.

Local buses may operate on evenings, weekends, and holidays. Some drivers work swing shifts, which means working for a few hours, taking a long break, then working a few more hours. The workdays of local drivers are usually eight hours.

Intercity bus drivers take people from city to city, from state to state, or across the country. If the trip is a very long one, two or more drivers

Bus transportation is important for many members of a community, including disabled people.

will share the long-distance route. When they get their assignment, drivers go to their buses and look them over to make sure that the buses pass safety checks.

Drivers greet passengers, collect tickets, and stow baggage. They help anyone who may need assistance entering the bus. They must leave on time and keep to the schedule. Most cross-country buses stop in many cities. The driver makes sure that people get off at the right place.

Intercity bus drivers must be able to make minor repairs if a problem comes up during a trip. If the bus has a serious problem or if an accident happens, the driver must be able to handle the situation. If the bus is disabled, the driver must call the company, which will provide another bus.

Intercity bus drivers must keep records of the amount of money received from passengers and the route driven. They must also fill out reports if an accident has occurred.

Intercity bus drivers must also keep track of the hours that they work and the number of miles that they drive. Laws limit the number of hours that intercity drivers may drive. They may drive ten hours at a time, but they must rest after eight hours. The most they can work in a week is sixty hours. Bus drivers for large companies often work fewer than forty hours a week. They often drive six to ten hours a day. Many have to work on weekends and holidays.

With experience, a local bus driver may become a long-distance intercity driver or a long-haul truck driver. Some drivers become supervisors or dispatchers. As intercity bus drivers work longer and gain experience, they can move up to better routes and raises in salary.

Outlook for Jobs

The future looks good for local bus drivers because cities are always trying to improve their local transit systems. More drivers will be needed, but there will be much competition for these jobs in the coming years.

The outlook for intercity bus drivers is fair. Bus companies have to compete with cars, trains, and airplanes for passengers. And since they pay so well, there is always competition for job openings. There are about 130,000 intercity bus drivers employed by 1,300 bus companies. That number is not expected to increase much in the coming years.

For more information on local bus drivers and intercity bus drivers, write to:

American Public Transit Association
1225 Connecticut Avenue, NW
Washington, DC 20036
(202) 828–2800

Transport Workers Union of America
80 West End Avenue
New York, NY 10023
(212) 873–6000

Interested people can also apply directly to bus companies. They should also check the classified ads in the newspapers.

Chapter 4
Seaman, Steward, and Cook

Many people think of a job at sea as an exciting adventure sailing over the ocean toward the horizon. But jobs at sea are difficult work. Ordinary seamen, able seamen, stewards, and cooks are workers in the Merchant Marine, the ships that carry freight. Ordinary seamen and able seamen are two different levels or classes of worker. The able seaman is the more experienced of the two.

Education, Training, and Salary

There are no formal education requirements for these jobs. People train for one year as ordinary seamen before they can become able seamen. To become certified as an able seaman, a sailor must be able to tie common knots, know how to handle all equipment and gear, and be familiar with all parts of the ship.

Ordinary and able seamen receive on-the-job training. However, it is very helpful if they already know about the sea when they come to the job. Many people serve in the Coast Guard or Navy before entering the Merchant Marine.

Labor unions run some schools to train ordinary seamen. Many seamen receive their papers by registering at union hiring halls, which are located at major ports.

There are also federal and state marine academies where new students can learn seamanship. Requirements for the job of ordinary seaman include being a U.S. citizen and having a recommendation from a union, ship's master, or steamship company. Seamen report to the hiring halls to see if there are job openings. The first openings go to the people with the most experience. As a result, beginning seamen may have to wait a long time to find openings.

Stewards and cooks must have seaman's papers and training for their jobs. Coast Guard or Navy experience and cook's training is useful. Training schools are available.

Ordinary seamen start at about $240 a week. Able seamen earn about $300 a week. Seamen of either class earn extra pay with overtime. When there are weeks without work, however, seamen do not get paid. Kitchen attendants and utility hands earn about $11,000 a year. Chief stewards and cooks earn from $16,000 to $18,000 a year. Benefits include room, meals, medical insurance, vacations, and retirement plans.

Job Description

Ordinary and able seamen work on land and at sea on passenger ships, freighters, and tankers. Able seamen handle the mooring lines when the ship comes into or leaves the dock. They take care of the deck equipment and gear. And they steer the ship, under the direction of their superior officer. Able seamen are responsible for standing watch when at sea. They must know all fire and safety rules. In an emergency, able seamen direct crewmates to lifeboats.

34

Cooks gain training aboard naval vessels.

Able seamen are also in charge of maintaining the ship, including painting and rust removal. Many are also skilled carpenters or electricians. They put these skills to work on the ship.

Ordinary seamen are like trainees, learning from the more experienced able seamen. They clean deck areas and crew quarters and operate some equipment. They may help able seamen with steering and the watch.

Stewards supervise food preparation, maintain mess halls and living quarters, and keep track of supplies. On passenger ships, stewards see that passengers have what they need. Ships' cooks prepare and serve all food and keep kitchens clean.

Outlook for Jobs

Seamen must pass a Coast Guard exam to move up to the next level. An ordinary seaman with one year's experience can apply for a limited endorsement. A seaman who is at least nineteen years old and has passed the exam can receive full endorsement. With experience, an able seaman can move up to become boatswain, supervising the deck crew. Cooks can advance to higher levels with experience and recommendations.

There may not be many jobs in the future for ordinary and able seamen, stewards, and cooks because of automation—more machines will be doing the work. There will be much competition for openings, so the seamen with the most experience will get the jobs.

This seaman is taking readings to give to the ship's navigator.

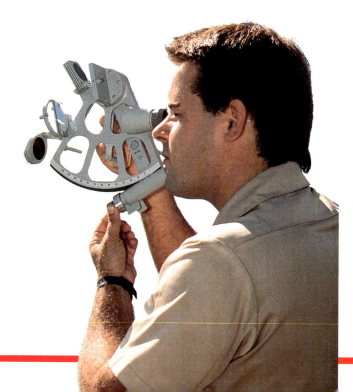

For more information on ordinary and able seamen, ship's stewards, and cooks, write to:

National Maritime Union of America
346 West 17th Street
New York, NY 10011
(212) 620–5700

Seafarers International Union of North America
5201 Auth Way
Camp Springs, MD 20746
(301) 899–0675

United Seamen's Service
One World Trade Center
New York, NY 10048
(212) 775–1033

Chapter 5
Railroad Braker and Conductor

People who take trains to work every day and travelers who take scenic train trips across the country enjoy smooth, comfortable, reliable travel thanks to railroad crews. Two of the workers on these crews are the railroad braker and the conductor.

Education, Training, and Salary

There is no education requirement for a railroad braker. High school education is required for the job of conductor.

Brakers learn on the job. As trainees, they go with experienced workers on many trips before they can work on their own. They must pass written tests on railroad procedures and rules. New brakers fill in for sick or vacationing workers. Brakers must be physically healthy and strong, with excellent eyesight and hearing. They must take physical exams throughout their careers to make sure they are healthy and can handle the job. Working as a braker is good training for a conductor's job.

Conductors with good records and the ability to deal well with people may move up to become passenger agents. These workers assist passengers with schedules and ticketing.

Most railroad brakers and conductors belong to unions. Brakers are paid by the mile or by the hour. They are paid more for runs of over 100 miles on freight trains and 150 miles on passenger trains. Brakers usually start at $30,000 a year. With experience, they can earn up to $45,000. Benefits include medical insurance, paid vacations, and retirement plans.

Conductors' salaries may depend on their railroad and their duties. They may be paid by the hour or the mile. Extra pay is given when conductors work dangerous routes, such as those through mountains. They can also get overtime pay. For safety, there is a limit to the number of miles or hours a conductor may work without rest.

Job Description

Some brakers work in railroad yards as yard couplers or helpers. Others work on trains. Yard brakers handle switches to connect and disconnect trains. They also operate hand brakes.

Brakers on passenger and freight trains operate warning lights and signals when the train is moving or stopping. Before the train leaves the station, the braker makes sure all equipment, tools, flares, and lanterns are fastened down. They must constantly check for danger signs such as sparks, smoke, brake problems, or broken equipment. They may be in charge of coupling (joining together) and uncoupling train cars if necessary.

Brakers often work nights, holidays, and weekends. They usually work a forty-hour workweek. For overtime, they get higher pay.

Conductors who work in the train yard are called *yard conductors.* They supervise the workers who put together and disconnect the many freight cars that make up a train. They may also handle the switches that control the track and trains.

Road conductors work on passenger or freight trains. Before the train leaves, the dispatcher gives the schedule and route to the conductor, who passes them on to the crew. Conductors check out all cars and make note of any repairs that may be needed. These repairs are taken care of before the train leaves the station. Conductors are also in charge of signaling the engineer when the train can pull out. While the train is making its run, the conductor is in charge. All workers on the train have to follow the conductor's orders.

On passenger trains, conductors are responsible for the crew and the passengers. They collect fares and answer passengers' questions. They may announce stops for passengers. Conductors must keep records on trips—the number of passengers, the schedule, or details about cargo on freight trains. They report to the train company.

Conductors are responsible for many tasks, including supervising other workers. They must be fully familiar with the way a train works. Those who work on passenger trains must deal with people courteously and helpfully.

One group of road conductors is called *extra board conductors.* Their schedules are more irregular. They are called on when the road conductor has worked the maximum number of consecutive hours.

41

At a glance

Passenger service   Yard conductor

↑   ↑

Yard and freight braker can move up to

Passenger service   Road service conductor

↑   ↑

Passenger train braker can move up to

Passenger agent   Trainmaster

↑   ↑

Conductor can move up to

Outlook for Jobs

Brakers have a couple of different choices when it is time to move up to a job with more responsibility and higher pay. Yard brakers can stay in the yard and become yard conductors. Or they can move to another branch of the railroad and work in passenger service. Passenger train brakers can advance to be road service conductors or go into passenger service.

Class I railroads, a group of the largest railroad companies, employ 27,000 brakers. With increased use of automated machinery to handle brakers' tasks, the number of jobs will not grow. But openings will come up when workers advance to other jobs or retire.

Today there are 42,000 conductors working on railroads. This number is expected to drop in the coming years. A big reason for this is the drop in the number of passengers who ride the trains. More electronic equipment will be used in the yards, which will reduce the need for yard conductors.

For more information on railroad brakers and conductors, write to:

Association of American Railroads
50 F Street, NW
Washington, DC 20001
(202) 639–2100

United Transportation Union
14600 Detroit Avenue
Lakewood, OH 44107
(216) 228–9400

Interested people should also apply directly to railroad employment offices.

Chapter 6
Mechanic

Most people depend on a variety of vehicles nearly every day. We expect our cars to start up when we need them to take us to our schools and jobs. We take buses and trains in town and out of state. We depend on airplanes for rapid traveling across the country or around the world. And we enjoy our recreational vehicles. The people responsible for keeping all these vehicles in good working order are mechanics.

Education, Training, and Salary

Mechanics should have a high school education. They must have mechanical ability to begin with. Given that start, they can learn the necessary skills for their particular job. High school courses in machine shop and auto repair are very helpful. Some math and science courses are also useful to a mechanic.

Aircraft mechanics usually attend a school approved by the Federal Aviation Administration (FAA). The course takes eighteen to twenty-four months. There are also FAA-approved courses in some high schools. Students then can take a mechanic's exam. Aircraft mechanics must get an A license or a P license. With an A license, mechanics can work on the body of an airplane. With a P license, they are able to work on the airplane's engine.

Auto mechanics can train on the job. Vocational schools and some community colleges also offer classes for auto mechanics. Some workers start out in gas stations.

Many boat mechanics learn on the job. They start out cleaning boats and motors and begin to do minor repairs. With two or three years' experience, they can become mechanics. They may also attend training courses.

Beginning diesel mechanics may train on the job for three to four years, assisting mechanics. They also can enroll in a trade or technical school for classroom and practical experience.

Aircraft mechanics start out at about $16,000 to $18,000 a year. Larger companies usually pay more, and mechanics with both A and P ratings earn more. Auto mechanics earn from $20,000 to $29,000, depending on experience and the difficulty of the work. Boat mechanics average $17,000 to $19,000. Some are paid hourly rates, and some work on a bonus system. In such a plan, the more work they do, the more they are paid. Diesel mechanics average $20,500 a year. All mechanics get benefits such as medical insurance, paid vacations, and retirement plans.

Job Description

There are many different types of mechanics. Aircraft mechanics service commercial airliners, private planes, and military aircraft. They inspect planes and do safety checks.

Some mechanics make minor repairs on planes before they take off. Others do major repairs at an airport's overhaul base. They specialize in one area of the plane.

46

Some aircraft mechanics work in general aviation shops, in smaller airports, and for private airplane charter firms. They must have good general knowledge and be able to fix all parts of a plane. Aircraft mechanics also work in manufacturing plants where planes are built. They get planes ready for test flights and make sure that the planes meet safety standards.

Automobile mechanics work on cars, buses, and trucks. They check cars and other vehicles for problems. They repair or replace parts to put the vehicle in good working order. Auto mechanics must be able to work on every part of a car, but some mechanics specialize.

Mechanics work for service stations, repair shops, and car dealers. They may be employed by taxicab companies, car rental agencies, or other firms with a fleet of cars as well. Some work for auto makers. They prepare cars for delivery to buyers or fix cars that customers bring in.

Auto mechanics often use electronic and computerized equipment to detect problems.

Boat mechanics repair small craft, fishing boats, or cabin cruisers. They work on inboard or outboard motors. Outboard motors are attached to the outside of small boats and can be removed easily. Inboard motors are inside larger boats and are only removed for major repairs.

Boat mechanics in small shops do many different jobs, from fixing motors to maintaining the outside of the boat. In larger shops, mechanics may specialize. They usually own their own hand tools, which can cost up to $400. They need to know how to use power tools and testing equipment. Some mechanics work at boat dealers or at marinas where boats are docked.

Airline mechanics are trained to spot and repair problems before they become life threatening.

Diesel mechanics fix diesel engines in trucks, buses, ships, trains, and other vehicles. Diesel engines are expensive to replace, so mechanics often take them apart and rebuild them or replace parts. Mechanics use hand tools, power tools, and testing equipment.

Outlook for Jobs

Mechanics can move up to be head mechanics or crew chiefs. Mechanics may become supervisors and maintenance superintendents. The Federal Aviation Administration (FAA) hires experienced aircraft mechanics as supervisors, managers, plant superintendents, or marine engineers. Some mechanics may start their own businesses.

The future looks good for mechanics in all areas. More auto mechanics will be needed to service cars with pollution-control devices, air-conditioning, and other extras that require maintenance. Boat mechanics will be needed to work on boats with more power features. The overall number of boats is growing each year because people have more time and money to spend on leisure. The number of diesel buses and trucks has more than doubled in the past twenty years, so diesel mechanics will be in demand.

For more information on mechanics, write to:

Automotive Service Industry Association
444 North Michigan Avenue
Chicago, IL 60611
(312) 836–1300

Aviation Maintenance Foundation
P.O. Box 2826
Redmond, VA 98073
(206) 823–0633

Diesel Engine Manufacturers Association
30200 Detroit Avenue
Cleveland, OH 44145-1967
(216) 899–0100

International Association of Machinists and Aerospace Workers
1300 Connecticut Avenue, NW
Washington, DC 20036
(202) 857–5200

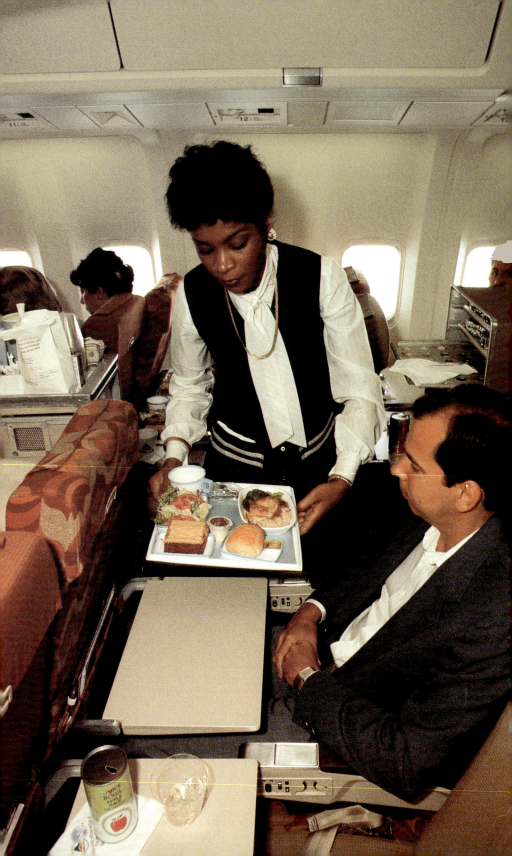

Chapter 7
Flight Attendant

Airline travel has become very common today. We fly on short trips to the next state or on longer trips to visit other countries. Business travelers depend on the airlines to get them to important meetings. And vacation travelers often choose airline travel for its speed and convenience. Many workers in the airline industry help make our trips possible. And one of these is the airline flight attendant.

Education, Training, and Salary

Flight attendants must have a high school education. Most companies require that these workers be at least nineteen years old. They need excellent vision and hearing, a good speaking voice, and good physical health.

Most airlines have their own training schools for flight attendants. Some do not have their own schools but send their employees to outside classes. Training programs usually run four to six weeks. In them, attendants learn requirements of the job, aircraft procedure, company policy, emergency guidelines, first aid, and other important subjects. Students also go on practice flights.

Flight attendants usually start out earning $14,800 a year. The average salary for flight attendants with experience is $23,000. When they are in training, flight attendants receive an allowance for rooms and meals. Once on the job, attendants need uniforms, which they must buy. Benefits include vacations and sick leave. Some airlines also provide medical insurance. Attendants also get discount plane fares for themselves and their families.

Job Description

Flight attendants fly on all major commercial airline flights. They are in charge of passengers' safety and comfort during the flight.

Before leaving the terminal, attendants must check all inside aircraft equipment and make sure food and supplies have been delivered. Attendants greet passengers as they board planes and help them find their seats. The attendant may also help passengers store coats or carry-on bags in safe places.

Attendants make sure passengers are seated with seat belts fastened before takeoff. They instruct passengers about what to do in an emergency. They check to see that emergency exits are not blocked and are tightly secured. For safety reasons, they sometimes have to move children seated near emergency exits.

When the plane has reached a certain altitude, flight attendants may begin showing a movie or serving meals. They also pass out magazines and stereo headphones to passengers who want them.

In case of an emergency, flight attendants are trained to react calmly and intelligently. They assist passengers by opening doors, inflating emergency slides, and giving first aid. There are many stories of brave flight attendants who put the passengers' safety before their own in emergencies.

The number of attendants on each flight may depend on the size of the plane and the number of passengers. Normally between one and ten attendants are on each flight. The largest aircraft may have up to sixteen.

Flight attendants are based in cities with major airports. This city is their home base. It may be San Francisco, Los Angeles, Chicago, Pittsburgh, Minneapolis, Newark, or another large city. Attendants for international airlines can be based in other countries.

Each month a flight attendant might have seventy-five to eighty hours of scheduled flight time and fifty hours of ground duty. They do not work regular workweeks, since many of their assignments are at night, on holidays, and on weekends. Most flight attendants get a total of fifteen days off each month.

Flight attendants meet all kinds of people in their work. They work very hard and are on their feet for many hours at a time. Yet they must try to smile and be polite to passengers throughout each trip. If it is a particularly busy time of the year, attendants may have flights scheduled back to back, with very little time off. They must often get by on little sleep and still perform their jobs well and cheerfully.

Many flight attendants enjoy working for airlines that fly worldwide. They must often speak foreign languages to work for those airlines. An international job means travel to many interesting and unusual places. This can be a fascinating job for those who choose it.

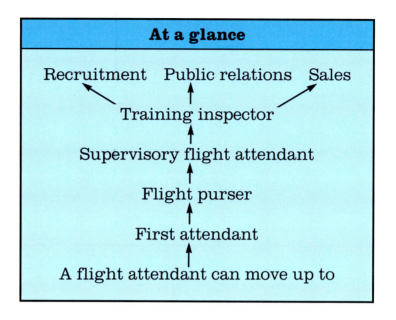

At a glance

Recruitment   Public relations   Sales

↑

Training inspector

↑

Supervisory flight attendant

↑

Flight purser

↑

First attendant

↑

A flight attendant can move up to

The life of a flight attendant with a family can be difficult. Attendants are often gone for long periods of time on a series of trips. But many say that the job and travel benefits are greater than the difficulties.

Outlook for Jobs

A flight attendant with experience can advance to be a first attendant, flight purser, supervisory flight attendant, and recruiter. Attendants may choose to go into another area of airline work, such as sales or public relations. Flight attendants with a few years' experience can choose their home bases and flights.

The future looks good for people interested in becoming flight attendants. The FAA requires that there be at least one attendant for every fifty seats on an aircraft. With more and larger planes in use, flight attendants will continue to be in demand. There will always be competition for these jobs because of the very good benefits. However, the economy can affect the amount of traveling people do. When the economy is slow, people cut down on the amount of flying.

For more information on airline flight attendants, write to:

Association of Flight Attendants
1625 Massachusetts Avenue, NW
Washington, DC 20036
(202) 328–5400

Independent Federation of Flight Attendants
630 Third Avenue
New York, NY 10017
(212) 818–1130

Interested people should also apply directly to airline companies for jobs. You can get a list of airline companies by writing to the Air Transport Association of America. Openings may be listed in the newspaper classified ads.

Chapter 8
Railroad Signaler, Telegrapher, Telephoner, and Dispatcher

Safe train travel depends on many things. It depends on well-kept, safe trains; skilled workers; and many mechanical features that most travelers do not see. Included in these important safety areas are the signaling, message, and switching systems of railroads. The workers who operate these systems are signalers, telegraphers, telephoners, and dispatchers.

Education, Training, and Salary

These railroad workers must have a high school education. High school shop courses in electricity and mechanics are very helpful. Math courses are also useful in these jobs. Some workers have technical school training. Workers must be between eighteen and thirty-five years old.

Workers just starting out work under experienced railroad workers to learn their jobs. They begin as assistants and learn about the rail system as well as the job's duties. Railroad telegraphers, telephoners, and dispatchers must pass a written exam and a practical test to prove that they know how to use the equipment and understand train procedures.

57

Railroad signalers earn between $32,000 and $35,000 a year. Telegraphers, telephoners, and dispatchers usually earn about $30,000 a year. Workers in all these jobs may receive time-and-a-half pay for overtime work. Benefits include train passes for free rides, medical insurance, paid vacations and holidays, and retirement plans.

Job Description

Train dispatchers may be hundreds of miles away, yet they can use signals to communicate with the crews on trains or in the yards. The workers who handle these signals are the railroad signalers. They put signals along the track and inside the train and keep them in working order. Signals may be electric switches or lights.

The signaler also hooks up the system that connects the signals to the dispatcher. Connections are made electrically or through microwave transmitters, depending on the distance. Signalers may be responsible for installing concrete or metal tower bases to hold the signals.

The workers who repair or replace broken parts of the signal system are the signal maintainers. They check out wires, switches, lights, and transmitters. Older mechanical systems with batteries are also checked out. Signal maintainers must fill out reports on all work completed.

Signalers and signal maintainers usually work outdoors in good weather and bad. They work a regular forty-hour week but may have to travel. Maintainers must always be ready to fix systems that fail without warning. The work can be dangerous. So signalers and signal maintainers must be careful.

Railroad telegraphers, telephoners, and dispatchers send important messages to the crews. They make sure that the tracks will be clear for the trains scheduled to use them. The ways these workers send messages are different.

The dispatchers may work controls that move switches and tracks by hand. Or they may use remote control to move them. They operate signals to keep trains on all tracks running smoothly.

Telegraphers and telephoners send messages from the dispatcher to the crew on the train. Messages must be clear at all times to make sure all workers are following the same plan.

Telegraphers, telephoners, and dispatchers generally work regular forty-hour weeks. They are limited by the law to no more than nine hours' work each day, except in emergencies. They work in busy offices, keeping track of many trains and systems at the same time.

Outlook for Jobs

Signalers and signal maintainers with experience and leadership ability can move up to be leading signalers or maintainers. They may also advance to become gang supervisors. Signal maintainers may be selected as testers or inspectors. Skilled workers can become signal engineers.

Railroad telegraphers, telephoners, and dispatchers who are just starting out are placed on an extra board. This means they will be called if an experienced worker is ill or takes a vacation. After they put in time and gain experience, new workers are given assignments when they open up. Telegraphers and telephoners may advance to become train dispatchers or agents.

Talking About the Job

Flashing lights are my business. I'm John Sanjusto, and I'm a signaler with the Sante Fe Railroad. I joke that lights are my business, but they are one of the most important parts of my job.

I work with wayside signals, the ones alongside the tracks, and with cab signals inside the trains. The thing many people don't understand is that train signals are much more complicated than, say, traffic lights at intersections. Ours aren't just go, slow down, and stop. We have more combinations of colors that mean different things, and train crews must know them well.

Signals tell crews what track to use or whether another train is up ahead. They also tell them if they have to switch tracks, whether they can go maximum speed, if they should prepare to stop, and other important things. They control traffic, the same way that traffic lights work.

Today these things are done with microcircuitry. As with stereos and tape recorders, signals started out large and now have gotten smaller and give better performance. To keep up with the changing technology, my company is training me to learn to use these new signals. I'm taking courses to update my knowledge and skills so I can work with the new systems. I find learning these new systems enjoyable. They help us react to things more quickly. They give us better control over signals.

We signalers are on call twenty-four hours a day and have to be ready to handle any emergencies that may come up, such as an ice storm or other severe weather. Switches in the yards often have heaters underneath them, but those outside the yards can, freeze up. The pieces of rail that are supposed to be switched do not move if they freeze. If you're riding a train, you might see workers out there lighting fires on the tracks trying to thaw the switches. If an emergency like this comes up, all signals go red for the engineer and crew. Trains are automatically stopped until the repairs are made. Things like this can come up anytime, so signalers have to be prepared day or night.

The future for signalers and signal maintainers looks better than it does for other railroad workers. There may be some growth in these jobs as workers are needed to work remote-controlled signals. And if rail freight business picks up, workers will be hired to handle signals for those.

Telegraphers, telephoners, and dispatchers may not find many job openings in the future. More message systems and mechanical operations will be electronically controlled. And many operations will be handled at a central location instead of at smaller, separate ones. This will cut down on the number of workers needed.

For more information on signalers, signal maintainers, telegraphers, telephoners, and dispatchers, write to:

Association of American Railroads
50 F Street, NW
Washington, DC 20001
(202) 639–2100

Brotherhood of Railroad Signalers
601 West Gold Road
Mt. Prospect, IL 60056
(708) 439–3732

United Transportation Union
14600 Detroit Avenue
Lakewood, OH 44107
(216) 228–9400

Interested people could also apply directly to the railroad companies. They could check with state employment offices as well.

Chapter 9
Merchant Marine Engineer

Imagine working in hot, cramped quarters with dangerous equipment for hours at a time. These are often the surroundings for Merchant Marine engineers. People who want to become engineers need a great deal of training in how a ship works. They provide an important service, maintaining our country's sea vessels.

Education, Training, and Salary

A high school education is required for Merchant Marine engineers. They have to pass very difficult tests, including the Coast Guard exam for engineers. They must know a lot about a ship's machinery, electricity, and other systems. They must also understand steam fitting, metal shaping, and assembly of parts. Passing this test gives the worker an engineer's license. Different tests are created for each level of engineer.

Most Merchant Marine engineers complete a training program before taking the exam. They train on diesel engines and marine steam systems. Some attend the Coast Guard Academy, Naval Academy, or Merchant Marine Academy. Others study at a state marine academy in California, Texas, Massachusetts, Maine, Michigan, or New York.

Some people without formal marine education may get jobs as Merchant Marine engineers. They must have at least three years of experience working in a ship's engine room and be at least nineteen years old. They have to pass a very difficult exam to be considered for the job.

The earnings of a Merchant Marine engineer depend on rank. A third assistant engineer can earn about $14,500 a year. A second assistant will earn $15,000 a year. A first assistant will earn about $16,500. Chief engineers earn $50,000 a year. If they work overtime, engineers get an extra 50 percent of their base pay. If they work overtime in port, they get overtime pay. Benefits include room, meals, various medical insurance programs, paid vacations, and retirement pensions.

Job Description

Merchant Marine engineers keep all of a ship's machinery in top running order. They work in the engine rooms of tankers, freighters, or passenger ships. Engineers live on the ship and are on call twenty-four hours a day to handle any situations that may come up.

Chief engineers are in charge of all seamen who work in the engineering area. They are responsible for the main power plant and the equipment that supports it. Chief engineers must keep track of all maintenance work on the ship's engine. Engines are complex machines. They must be maintained regularly.

Below the chief engineer are three levels of assistants. The first assistant engineer is the

This engineer is looking at the engine's gauges to make sure that all pressure levels are correct.

highest level. The third assistant engineer is the lowest. The first assistant engineer's job is to start up the engines, stop them, and make sure that they are all running properly and at the correct speed. The second assistant is in charge of boilers, pumps, and all water and fuel.

The third assistant handles the lubrication system. He or she may also be responsible for the ship's refrigeration system and electrical equipment. Other workers are needed in the engine room area as well. Oilers lubricate all moving parts in the equipment. Water tenders and firers check the oil and water in boilers and oil-burning equipment. And wipers clean the machinery and the rest of the engine room area. These workers do not need to pass the engineer's license test. These jobs may be a way to get initial experience.

Merchant Marine engineers travel on the ship much of the time. They live in small quarters and usually work in shifts. They may work eight hours on duty, with eight hours off. They normally work regular forty-hour weeks when they are in port.

Outlook for Jobs

Merchant Marine assistant engineers can move up to higher ranks by gaining experience and successfully passing the test for the next level. Labor unions have training programs that can help workers pass exams.

After third assistant engineers work one year, they can move up to the position of second assistant engineer. They must be at least twenty-one years old and must take the Coast Guard exam to qualify for the next rank. Second assistant engineers must take Coast Guard exams to advance to first assistant engineer. Another set of exams is needed to move up to the position of chief engineer.

The job outlook is fair for people interested in becoming Merchant Marine engineers. It is predicted that the Merchant Marine fleet will increase up to the year 2000. But with more automation, there will be fewer jobs for workers aboard ships. As a result, there will be a lot of competition for those jobs.

For more information on Merchant Marine engineers, write to:

National Board of Boiler and Pressure Vessel Inspectors
1055 Crupper Avenue
Columbus, OH 43229
(614) 888–8320

National Marine Engineers Beneficial Association
444 North Capitol
Washington, DC 20001
(202) 347–8585

National Maritime Union of America
346 West 17th Street
New York, NY 10011
(212) 620–5700

Seafarers International Union of North America
5201 Auth Way
Camp Springs, MD 20746
(301) 899–0675

Interested people should check at their school placement office for information on marine academies. They may also write to their representative in Congress for information.

Chapter 10
Car or Truck Rental Agent

People sometimes need to rent a car or truck. They may rent cars for long trips or while their own cars are being serviced. Trucks of all sizes are rented for moving furniture and other large items, or for hauling supplies or materials. The people in charge of matching up customers and vehicles are car and truck rental agents.

Education, Training, and Salary

A high school education is required for a full-time job as a car or truck rental agent. Car leasing companies, which rent cars for a year or longer, require agents to have at least one year of sales experience. Some require college courses.

Car and truck rental agencies train their employees either on the job or in company training programs.

Car rental agents' salaries depend on the area of the country. Beginning rental agents start at from $9,000 to $15,500 a year.

Truck rental agents may be paid from $4.00 to $6.00 per hour plus commission or at about $13.00 an hour without a commission.

Car leasing companies generally pay agents between $17,000 and $21,000 a year. Some agents work on salary plus commission.

Job Description

People come to car and truck rental agents to rent vehicles for a day or longer. Car rental agents may work for small independent rental agencies or large national companies. Rental agencies are located on main streets in towns or cities, or at airports, train stations, and bus terminals.

Business travelers often rent cars while they are in a city for meetings. Vacationers may rent a car to use when they arrive at their destination. Some people who live in very large cities do not own cars; they rely on public transportation. When they need to go out of town, however, they often rent a car. And if someone's car is in the shop for repairs, the owner may turn to daily car rentals to have a car while the repairs are made.

Car rental agents help people choose the car that is right for their needs. Most reservations are made by phone, but some are made in person. Agents ask the customer what size car they think they will need and for how many days. The agents must be familiar with the differences among the rental company's cars and with the different rental rates for each type of car. They ask customers whether they wish to purchase collision insurance and when they will be picking up the car. They explain whether the rental rate includes free mileage or not.

Agents have customers fill out the necessary forms, including a rental agreement. This states the price, the car model, the mileage allowance, and other information. Customers must show a driver's license and pay a deposit on the car.

If a customer wants to pick up a car in one city and drop it off in another, the agent must make arrangements for this. The mileage and total rental fees are figured out when the customer turns in the car. Agents also check returned cars to make sure they are in good condition.

Rental companies have two other types of workers. Customer service representatives take care of complaints or other problems customers may have. Station managers supervise car rental agents and oversee all that goes on in the office.

Leasing agents handle long-term rentals to people who will need one car or truck or a fleet of cars for a longer period of time. Many companies lease cars instead of buying them since leasing companies pay for repairs and maintenance. Leased cars may also be a benefit provided to high-level employees. Customers usually pay a monthly charge for the use of the car.

Leasing agents for large companies may work in regional sales offices in different parts of the country. Others may work in leasing depart-

THE TOP TEN CAR RENTAL COMPANIES IN SALES		
Company	Sales (in millions)	U.S. Locations
Hertz Corporation	$2,900	1,500
Avis Rent a Car System Inc.	2,500	1,400
National Car Rental System Inc.	2,200	850
Budget Rent a Car Corp.	1,800	1,228
Dollar Rent A Car Systems Inc.	700	740
Alamo Rent A Car Inc.	440	80
Enterprise Rent A Car	400	450
American Int'l Rent A Car Corp.	350	104
Thrifty Rent-A-Car System Inc.	239	360
Agency Rent A Car	227	550

ments of car dealers. They are supervised by sales managers and regional managers.

Some truck rental agencies specialize in renting moving trucks or heavy equipment for construction. Truck rental firms sometimes hire part-time employees to rent vehicles. Rental agents must know about different sizes of trucks and how they operate.

Car and truck rental agents work behind counters or in offices, dealing with customers. They must be helpful and polite and provide good service so that customers will return. The way they treat customers is very important to the success of the rental business. There is great competition for customers, so agencies must do what they can to win their loyalty.

Agents need to be well informed about their company's policies. They need to keep up to date on special rates and promotions.

Outlook for Jobs

Car or truck rental agents can advance to higher levels if they have useful experience and deal well with customers. Agents can become station managers or supervisors at an agency. Or they may move up to be customer service representatives. With more experience, a representative can be promoted to a training department in a large leasing company.

Car leasing agents can advance to become sales managers and district managers. Some are promoted to management jobs in the main offices of leasing companies.

Car and truck rental is an excellent field for young people to enter. There will be many new job openings in the coming years, with existing agencies growing fast and new branches expected to start up. Of course, more openings will also arise as employees transfer to other jobs or retire.

For more information on car and truck rental agents, write to:

American Automotive Leasing Association
1001 Connecticut Avenue, NW
Washington, DC 20036
(202) 223–2118

International Brotherhood of Teamsters,
  Chauffeurs, Warehousemen and Helpers
  of America
25 Louisiana Avenue, NW
Washington, DC 20001
(202) 624–6800

Interested people should also apply directly to car and truck rental firms for jobs. They should check newspaper classified ads for openings.

73

Chapter 11
Airplane Pilot

Many people depend on aircraft for speedy and reliable service: businesspeople, vacationers, farmers, hospitals, airplane manufacturers, and safety organizations. We look to skilled pilots to operate the planes safely.

Education, Training, and Salary

A high school education is required to be a pilot. Some employers want applicants with college degrees.

Pilots may be trained in armed forces flight programs or in private flying schools. In the United States about 1,400 schools certified by the FAA offer pilot training.

People interested in becoming pilots must be at least seventeen years old and work toward getting a private pilot's license. They must take a physical exam and get twenty-five hours of flying experience. They must also pass a written test and a flying test to prove they have knowledge of a plane's instruments.

People must be at least eighteen years old with 250 hours of flying time to work toward a commercial pilot's license. They must take a physical exam, a written test, and a flying test. A commercial license is given for a certain class of aircraft. This could include single-engine planes, double-engine planes, or seaplanes.

75

Pilots must meet other requirements as well, such as an instrument rating to fly in bad weather, when the pilot cannot depend on sight. To receive this rating, a pilot must have forty hours of instrument flying experience.

To fly an airliner, people must receive an instrument rating and an airline transport pilot's license. They must be at least twenty-three years old and have 1,500 hours of flying time. Commercial pilots also need a restricted radio operator's license from the Federal Communications Commission (FCC).

Pilots' salaries depend on the type of plane they fly. Airline pilots average about $70,000 per year. Pilots who fly for private companies earn between $29,000 and $40,000. In general, pilots of jet planes earn more than pilots of nonjets.

Job Description

There are many different kinds of pilots, who operate a variety of planes. Whatever the type of plane they fly, all pilots are responsible for flying the aircraft and supervising their crew. They must always keep in mind the passengers' safety. And they are responsible for any freight they may be transporting.

Commercial airline pilots fly planes that carry passengers and cargo. They have many jobs to perform once they enter the cockpit area of the aircraft. They must check all controls, weather, and flight conditions. They read flight plans, which must be approved by the control tower.

The person who assists the pilot is the copilot. The copilot plans the route and figures out the flying time from one city to the next. The pilot must get the dispatcher's OK to begin moving, or taxiing, to the runway. At this point, the pilot may decide to have the plane checked once more. If not, the plane is ready for takeoff.

Commercial jetliners fly by automatic pilot once they are in the air. Air-route control stations keep in radio contact with the cockpit. Pilots report any problems, such as weather conditions, to the station. When the flight is completed, pilots must ready the aircraft to land. They make sure that landing gear is operating correctly and ask the air-traffic controllers for permission to land. The pilot then takes the plane down to a safe landing.

There are also other kinds of pilots. Agricultural pilots operate crop dusters that help fertilize crops. Some aid in putting out forest fires. Some fly planes for corporations.

Test pilots are hired by the FAA or by large airlines to check the performance and safety of airplanes. So-called check pilots fly with other pilots to make sure they are qualified. And helicopter pilots may report on traffic for radio or television stations, provide medical airlifts, or fly people to airports or other locations.

Outlook for Jobs

Pilots usually train as copilots before they are given their own assignments. Some begin as flight engineers, who maintain the cockpit instruments as well as the aircraft. With experience and years of service, pilots may get more desirable routes and raises in pay. Some pilots may decide to start up their own flying schools. Others may move to administrative jobs with large airlines.

77

Talking About the Job

I'd rather be in the air than anywhere else. And I've wanted to fly for as long as I can remember. My name is Elizabeth Westman, and I'm a pilot for a private company called the Apex Corporation.

I fly the president and some executives of the company all over the world to appointments and business meetings. Sometimes I have to be ready to pick up and go at a moment's notice. They might schedule a last-minute conference or plant visit— they have several manufacturing plants in Europe that they visit on a regular basis to check production.

My favorite assignment was to fly to Singapore. I had never been to the Far East before, and it was a real education for me. I learned so much about a different culture. I would have paid them to go!

This can be a hard job if you have a family. I'm single, so it works for me. But I think if I had a family it would be diffi-cult not to have regular hours and a normal schedule.

When I decided for sure in high school that I wanted to become a professional pilot, I looked into a couple of flight schools I had read about. I started by taking flying lessons on weekends to make sure this was for me. I really fell in love with flying the first time I flew solo.

So, after graduation I signed up for a full-time program at a flight school. Studying and learning all about aircraft was a lot of work. But I told myself that if I wanted it, I was going to have to work for it. And when they handed me my private pilot's license, I knew I was on my way.

I got a part-time job to support myself and I just kept flying until I had enough hours to go for a commercial license. I passed all the tests and the rest is history. When people ask me what I do, I just say, "I cruise the sky."

The future looks good for those interested in becoming professional pilots. There will always be competition for these jobs, but plenty of openings should be available. Among others, private businesses and agricultural firms are expected to be hiring pilots.

For more information on pilots, write to:

Aircraft Owners and Pilots Association
421 Aviation Way
Frederick, MD 21701
(301) 695–2000

Air Line Pilots Association International
1625 Massachusetts Avenue, NW
Washington, DC 20036
(202) 797–4000

Air Transport Association of America
1709 New York Avenue, NW
Washington, DC 20006
(202) 626–4000

Federal Aviation Science and Technological Association
285 Dorchester Avenue
South Boston, MA 02127
(617) 268–5002

Future Aviation Professionals of America
4959 Massachusetts Boulevard
Atlanta, GA 30337
(800) JET–JOBS

Interested people also can check with flight schools for more information.

Chapter 12
Getting the Job: Tips for the Reader

Starting Out

Whatever job you decide to go after, you want to do it to the best of your ability. And you can do this only if you have picked a job you enjoy and feel comfortable with. Be honest with yourself and begin your job search by knowing your talents and interests.

Rate Your Strengths

Write down on a piece of paper a few lines about yourself: what you like, what you dislike, what your favorite subject at school is, what your least favorite subject is, what bores you, what excites you.

Make a chart and list any jobs you have ever had. Include your supervisor's names, your work addresses, and the dates of employment. Now make a list of your hobbies or interests. Also list the schools you have attended and your extracurricular activities. This list would include clubs or teams you belong to. If you have done any volunteer work, be sure to list it. Finally, add to your list the names of any awards or prizes you have won. All this information helps you identify your strengths.

List Your Job Possibilities

List all the jobs in this book that sound interesting. Look at each job and see if you qualify. If a job you like requires extra training, write that down. Also check the publications in the back of this book and note the titles of any books or other materials that will tell you more about the jobs you like.

Look at your job list and your strengths list. See where they match up, and put a star by those jobs that would use your strengths.

Consult Counselors

Talk to a guidance counselor at your school about jobs that are open in your field of interest. Your state or local employment service can also help you.

Looking for Work

When you have settled on the jobs you would like, start looking for openings. Apply for as many jobs as you can—the more you apply for, the better your chance of finding one.

Research Find out everything you can about jobs you are applying for. The more information you have about jobs, employers, and employers' needs, the more impressive you will be in your interview.

Ads There are two types of newspaper classified ads: *help wanted* and *situation wanted*. A help wanted ad is placed by an employer looking for a worker to fill a specific job. It tells you the job, requirements, salary, company, and whom to contact. Or it is a blind ad, one that just has a post office box number. Answer the ad by letter or by phone, as directed in the ad. Follow up within two weeks with another phone call or letter if you have not heard from the employer.

A person looking for work can place a *situation wanted* ad. This ad tells the kind of work the person is looking for, why he or she qualifies, and when he or she could start working.

Networking   Networking is letting everyone know what jobs you're looking for. Talk to people in your field of interest, friends, or relatives who might be able to help. Some good leads on jobs can be found this way. Follow up on what you learn with a phone call or letter.

Employment Services   Check with the high school's or vocational school's placement service for job openings. State and local employment services often have job listings.

Classified Ads Help Wanted

Airline Miami Openings • General Mechanic • Machinists • A & P Hangar Work in engine service center, aircraft service center, or accessory service center. For interview call 1-800-555-5555. An Equal Opportunity Employer. **SUNBELT AIRWAYS, INC.**

AUTOMOTIVE TECHNICIANS Auto Fixit offers you the opportunity to develop your skills in a small business. Candidate should have experience in diagnosing and repairing brakes, steering, heating and air-conditioning, engine tuning, or electrical systems. Opportunities throughout the Greater Houston area. Call 555-4444 and ask for Mr. Gonzalez.

Does an adventure at sea sound exciting to you? See the world as a ship's steward or cook and earn good money. Will train. Must be 18 years old. Send letter to M. Rubenstein, 988 W. La Costa, San Lagos 90010.

Abbreviations

People who place classified ads often use abbreviated words to make an ad as short as possible. Read the classified ad section in your newspaper to become familiar with abbreviations. Here is a short list to help you now:

excel	excellent
bnfts.	benefits
exp	experience
p.t. or p/t	part time
h.s.	high school
grad	graduate
w.	with
avail.	available
f.t. or f/t	full time
emp.	employment
gd.	good
refs.	references
ext.	extension
req.	required
sal.	salary

Civil Service   Federal, state, and local governments offer some jobs in transportation. Find the civil service office near you and inquire. See the feature on the top of the next page. It explains more about civil service exams.

Unions   Find out about labor unions that may be involved with jobs in the field of community services. Check with union locals in your town; you can find phone numbers in the phone book.

Civil Service

Federal and state governments employ several million workers. In order to get a government job, you must first check with the Federal Job Information Center or a state department of personnel office for an announcement concerning the type of job that interests you. The announcement describes the job as well as the education and experience that all applicants will need to be qualified for the job.

Once you know about a government job opening, you must fill out an application to take a civil service test. If your application is approved, you must then take and pass the exam. Exams are usually written, but may also be oral. Some exams include essays or performance tests. Each exam is tailored to fit a specific job. An exam may cover such items as English usage, reasoning, or clerical or mechanical skills.

Temporary Employment   Working on a temporary basis can lead to other jobs or to part-time or full-time work.

Applying in Person

Applying to a company in person can be a good idea. Call for an appointment and tell the human resources officer that you would like to have an interview. Some employers may ask that you send a letter or résumé first.

Sending Letters

Writing letters to companies can be an effective way to ask about jobs. Typed letters are preferred, but neat, handwritten letters are acceptable. Check the yellow pages or industry magazines at the public library for companies' addresses. The reference librarian can help you. Address letters to the company's personnel or human resources department. Send your résumé with the letter. Keep copies of all letters and follow up in a couple of weeks with another letter or phone call.

Résumé

A résumé is a useful one-page outline of information about you that introduces you to a possible future employer. Based on your strengths list, it summarizes your education, work history, and skills.

You will enclose your résumé in letters you write future employers. You also will take it with you to give to your interviewer. Look at the sample résumé on page 87 to see how a typical résumé looks.

Always put your full name, address, and phone number at the top of the résumé. Type the résumé, if possible, or write it by hand neatly. Then state your objective, or the job you are applying for. Put down any experience that shows you are a good worker. Volunteer work and part-time jobs tell an employer that you are always looking to help out and work hard. Put down your most recent job first.

Finally, include information about your education. You can also list any special skills, awards, or honors you have received.

Writing Letters

When you send your résumé in the mail, always attach a cover letter. Your letter will be short, no

Tate Baker
1515 West Main Street
Flint, MI 55555
(313) 555-9790

Objective: To work as a car rental agent.

Experience
1989–   VARGAS USED CARS, Ogonta, MI
present   Part-time helper at used car lot.
             Assisted salespeople, learned duties.

1987–   U-TOW-IT TRUCK RENTAL, Towanda,
1988   MI
             Worked after school and evenings
             renting all sizes of trucks and vans.
             Filled out rental agreements, checked
             vehicles in and out. Handled insurance
             forms.

1985–   BOB'S CAR WASH CITY, South Bay, MI
1986   Worked after school and weekends
             washing and waxing cars, cleaning
             interiors, and collecting money. Was
             promoted to shift supervisor in charge
             of four employees.

Education
1989   Graduated FBC Vocational School,
             Rainer, MI

Present   Currently enrolled in Shawnee
             Community College Evening Session
             business class.

References enclosed.

more than two or three paragraphs. It should come right to the point and lead the employer to your résumé.

Explain what job you are interested in, and include a short listing of your qualifications. Your letter should catch the employer's interest so that the employer wants to turn to your résumé. See the sample on page 89.

Completing the Application Form

You may have to fill out an application form when applying for a job. (See the sample on pages 90 and 91.) This form asks for your education, experience, and other information.

The employer may mail an application form to you ahead of time or you may be asked to fill it out when you come for the interview.

Follow the instructions carefully and print or type information neatly. Neatness tells the employer that you care about work, can organize information, and can think clearly.

Have all information with you when you arrive. You may have to fill in salaries for past jobs, your social security number, the dates you worked, and your past supervisors' names, addresses, and phone numbers.

List your most recent jobs first, as you do on your résumé.

However, do not answer any question that you feel invades your privacy. Laws prevent an employer from asking about race, religion, national origin, age, marital status, family situation, property, car, or arrest record. Unless the question applies directly to the job, you do not have to answer it. (See "Know Your Rights.")

September 22, 1991
Cynthia R. Bongard
111 Center Street
Manchester, NJ 44444

Mr. William Raynor
Transwest Bus Lines
Transwest Plaza
Bloomington, RI 22222

Dear Mr. Raynor:

I am looking for a job as a short- or long-distance bus driver. I know that Transwest has a trainee program, and I am interested in applying for admission.

I am twenty-one years old, with an excellent driving record. I am in very good health, with perfect vision and hearing. I am a hard worker and eager to learn.

I would appreciate the opportunity to meet with you and show you some personal recommendations I have received in the past. I will call back in a week to see if we might set up an appointment. Thank you in advance for your time.

Sincerely,

Cynthia R. Bongard

enclosure

APPLICATION FOR EMPLOYMENT

(Please print or type your answers)

PERSONAL INFORMATION   Date _____

Name _____ Social Security Number _____ / _____ / _____

Address _____
        Street and Number   City   State   Zip Code

Telephone number (_____) _____ – _____ (_____) _____ – _____
                              day   evening

Job applied for _____ Salary expected $ _____ per _____

How did you learn of this position? _____

Do you want to work _____ Full time or _____ Part time?

Specify preferred days and hours if you answered part time _____

Have you worked for us before? _____ If yes, when? _____

On what date will you be able to start work? _____

Have you ever been convicted of a crime, excluding misdemeanors and summary offenses?

_____ No   _____ Yes

If yes, describe in full _____

Whom should we notify in case of emergency?

Name _____ Relationship _____

Address _____
        Street and number   City   State   Zip Code

Telephone number (_____) _____ – _____ (_____) _____ – _____
                              day   evening

EDUCATION

Type of School	Name and Address	Years Attended	Graduated	Course or Major
High School			Yes No	
College			Yes No	
Post-graduate			Yes No	
Business or Trade			Yes No	
Military or other			Yes No	

WORK EXPERIENCE (List in order, beginning with most recent job)

Dates		Employer's Name and Address	Rate of Pay Start/Finish	Position Held	Reason for Leaving
From	To				

ACTIVITIES AND HONORS (List any academic, extracurricular, civic, or other achievements you consider significant.)

_____

_____

PERSONAL REFERENCES

_____

Name and Occupation	Address	Phone Number

_____

_____

_____

PLEASE READ THE FOLLOWING STATEMENTS CAREFULLY AND SIGN BELOW:

The information that I have provided on this application is accurate to the best of my knowledge and is subject to validation. I authorize the schools, persons, current employer, and other organizations or employers named in this application to provide any relevant information that may be required to arrive at an employment decision.

_____   _____

Applicant's Signature   Date

The Interview

How you present yourself in a job interview will tell the employer a lot about you. It can be the biggest single factor that helps an employer decide whether to hire you.

Before you go to the interview, sit down and prepare what you will say. Think of why you want the job, your experience, and why you qualify. Know as much about the job and the company as possible through ads, brochures, or employees. This will show that you are interested in the company's needs.

Make a list of questions you have. And try to guess what the interviewer will ask. You may ask if you can work overtime or if you can take courses for more training or education. Bring in any certificates or licenses you may need to show.

Dress neatly and appropriately for the interview. Make sure you know exactly where the interview will take place so you will be on time. Allow extra time to get there in case you are delayed by traffic or for some other reason.

Following Up

After the interview, thank the interviewer for his or her time and shake hands. If the job appeals to you, tell the person that you are interested.

When you get back home, send a letter thanking the interviewer for his or her time. Repeat things that were discussed in the interview. Keep a copy of it for yourself and start a file for all future letters.

Think about how you acted in the interview. Did you ask the right questions? Were your answers right? If you feel you should have done something differently, make notes so you can do better the next time.

If you do not hear from the company in two weeks, write a letter to the interviewer repeating your interest. You can also phone to follow up.

Know Your Rights: What Is the Law?

Federal Under federal law, employers cannot discriminate on the basis of race, religion, sex, national origin, ancestry, or age. People aged forty to seventy are specifically protected against age discrimination. Handicapped workers also are protected. Of course, these laws protect only workers who do their job. Employers may refuse to hire workers who are not qualified and may fire workers who do not perform.

State Many states have laws against discrimination based on age, handicap, or membership in armed services reserves. Laws differ from state to state. In some states, there can be no enforced retirement age. And some protect people suffering from AIDS.

Applications When filling out applications, you do not have to answer questions that may discriminate. Questions about whether you are married, have children, own property or a car, or have an arrest record do not have to be answered. An employer may ask, however, if you have ever been convicted of a crime.

At Work It is against the law for employers to discriminate against workers when setting hours, workplace conditions, salary, hirings, layoffs, firings, or promotions. And no employer can treat a worker unfairly if he or she has filed a discrimination suit or taken other legal action.

Read Your Contract   Read any work contract you are given. Do not sign it until you understand and agree to everything in it. Ask questions if you have them. If you have used an employment agency, before you sign a contract, settle on whether you pay the fee for finding a job or the employer does.

When Discrimination Occurs: What You Can Do

Government Help   Call the Equal Employment Opportunity Commission or the state civil rights commission if you feel you've been discriminated against. If they think you have been unfairly treated, they may take legal action. If you have been unfairly denied a job, you may get it. If you have been unfairly fired, you may get your job back and receive pay that is owed you. Any mention of the actions taken against you may be removed from your work records. To file a lawsuit, you will need a lawyer.

Private Help   Private organizations like the American Civil Liberties Union (ACLU) and the National Association for the Advancement of Colored People (NAACP) fight against discrimination. They can give you advice.

Sources

General Career Information

Career Information Center, 4th ed. 13 vols. Mission Hills, Calif.: Glencoe/Macmillan, 1990.

Harrington, Thomas, and O'Shea, Arthur (eds.). *Guide for Occupational Exploration.* Circle Pines, Minn.: American Guidance Service, 1984.

Hopke, William E., et al. (eds.). *The Encyclopedia of Career and Vocational Guidance,* 7th ed., 3 vols. Chicago: Ferguson, 1987.

U.S. Department of Labor. *Occupational Outlook Handbook.* Washington, D.C.: U.S. Government Printing Office. Revised biennially.

Transportation

Airline Employees Association. *Your Airline Career.* Chicago: Airline Employees Association, 1983.

Green, Elizabeth A. *The Modern Conductor.* Englewood Cliffs, N.J.: Prentice-Hall, 1987.

Hammer, Hy (ed.) *Bus Operator.* New York: Arco, 1984.

Parados, Adrian A. *Opportunities in Transportation.* Skokie, Ill.: VGM Career Horizons, 1983.

Petersen, Gwenn B. *Careers in the United States Merchant Marine.* New York: Lodestar Books, 1983.

Weber, Robert. *Opportunities in Automotive Service.* Skokie, Ill.: VGM Career Horizons, 1983.

95

Index